January 2013

LOSING, FINDING

To Diana and Christian,
a memory, of Michael in these
'Sixteen Songs'.
With happy memories of us all
together in years gone by.

Wanda

For Jeeda and Imy

Also by Wanda Barford
Sweet Wine and Bitter Herbs
A Moon at the Door

LOSING, FINDING

Wanda Barford

IN ASSOCIATION WITH THE EUROPEAN JEWISH PUBLICATION SOCIETY

First published in England in 2002 by Flambard Press
Stable Cottage, East Fourstones, Hexham NE47 5DX
in association with the European Jewish Publication Society

The European Jewish Publication Society is a registered
charity which gives grants to assist in the publication
and distribution of books relevant to Jewish literature,
history, religion, philosophy, politics and culture.
EJPS, PO Box 19948, London N3 3ZJ.
Website: www.ejps.org.uk

Typeset by Harry Novak
Cover design by Gainford Design Associates
Printed in England by Cromwell Press, Trowbridge, Wiltshire

Flambard Press wishes to thank Northern Arts
for its financial support.

Website: www.flambardpress.co.uk

CONTENTS

Sixteen Songs for Michael

About Silence

From Childhood Tongues

SIXTEEN SONGS
FOR MICHAEL

Seulete suy, et seulete vueil estre.
Seulete m'a mon doulz ami laissiée.

Christine de Pizan (1364–1431)

ON WAKING

'Good Morning,' I still say to you,
Though there's no morning where you are
(But do we know it's true?).
'Good Morning,' I will say to you,
Hoping for a chink of blue
From a caring, distant star.
'Good Morning,' I'll still say to you,
Though there's no morning where you are.

LOOKING IN

The jasmine's reached your window now;
it presses its white flowers against the pane,
as if to say we do,
we do remember you;
you haven't lived in vain.

BURNT

'... the real bones
still undergoing everything.'
    Ted Hughes, *Birthday Letters*

Would that your bones
were still undergoing everything:
worm-bite, crumble, damp-swell, rot,
so I could still relate to you
in life-as-change, as it always is;
not this ghoulish, man-wreaked
transfiguration to ash.

Did your heart burn easily?
(They say Shelley's wouldn't.)
And the chiselled profile
I secretly admired in your corner
under the light, did it burn?
And your knee-bones
as they protruded further
abandoned by their covering of flesh?

And how did that fire compete
with the Zimbabwean sun's
that tanned your golden skin
as you lay lizard-like on a rock
by your stretch of the Hunyani river?

And your strong, Yorkshire, maker's hands
that built, planed, painted, planted,
whose fingers the disease emaciated
to over-sensitive digits
which were not you; did they burn?

And did the flames attack your hair
still abundantly covering
a just visible bald patch; hair
stubbornly shiny after its last shampoo,
and soft as a baby's when I combed it through?

SHOES

Today I sent off all your shoes to charity
(including shoe-trees, horns, loose inner soles),
the barge-like ones you paddled in when you had gout,
some snakeskin pumps, thin-soled, that pinched your feet;

a pair of grey ones bought to match your furry hat,
two formal pairs for trudging city streets,
and boots still new, your ankles felt rejected in;
blue moccasins that wrapped each foot in love.

To toe-and-heel the pedal-board with nimble touch,
you had some quasi winkle-pickers. They went.
(The diapason bellowed out its thunderous notes
when you played at other, distant funerals...)

I gave away your sandals – dusty, down-at-heel
(I see them climbing the Matopo Hills),
safari boots you took to Addis Ababa
to go up-country, check tobacco plants.

You quickstepped me, foxtrotted round the shiny floor
in 'co-respondent', patent leather shoes
that zigzagged, glided, formed the figure eight.
I kept them to the last, your bedroom slippers too.

CHATTERING

I'd love to phone you
and tell you what's been happening
over here – how I've cleaned
and tidied up your office
so you'd hardly recognise it
and thrown out eight bin-liners full;
how I haven't spent all your money;
how I've rearranged the garden,
planted grass and a herbaceous border
to make it look more English, more like you;
how I've tried to project my voice
when reading, not to drop it
at the end of sentences; how your
five-year-old grandson often says,
'Papa's dead, isn't he?', as if trying
to make sense of 'dead'; how we still
say grace before meals.

But here I go, I'm talking too much,
spending too long on the phone again.
Goodness knows what the cost will be
over such a long distance…

CHARADE

I'd love to call you back for Christmas Day
to spend some time at home with all of us,
and sit in your blue armchair with a rug.
If you're too weak and tired there'll be no need
to join in all the readying and the fuss.

We'd bring your meal laid neatly on a tray:
a glass of *Entre-Deux-Mers*, stuffed turkey breast,
few sprouts but showers of peas; and potatoes?
'Just one.' A mound of Christmas pud with rum,
'no brandy butter' you'd shout with zest.

You'd deck your head with gaudy paper hats
or any crown-like band or coloured frill.
Your presents we'd place down beside your chair;
you'd open them with all the air of one
who's much surprised to be remembered still.

Then shuffle over to the piano-stool,
and with that waggish, mock-heroic grin,
your now thin fingers with legato touch,
eyes staring at some inner youthful choir,
you'd let your carol repertoire begin…

oblivious of requests from those around:
'May we have … we'd like to sing … Daddy, play…'
And after dinner when we'd have charades
you'd don a sheet and be the attic ghost,
then out of breath, unnoticed slip away.

IT'S YOUR BIRTHDAY, I VISIT
KENSAL GREEN CEMETERY

Is this all that's left of you
Now they've burnt you through and through?
These small ashes in an urn
Brownish, rusting in its turn.

Is there really nothing more?
Nothing left of that great store:
Flesh and muscle, bone and brain,
Nerve and sinew, yes, and pain...

Thoughts of yours now lodge in me,
Teach me how to act and be.
(But I'd rather have you there
Resting in your blue armchair.)

I am tired of heaving round
How you looked, how you would sound...
'Happy Birthday' (loud) I say,
Empty-handed walk away.

KOSHER ANGLICAN

In hospital you ordered Kosher food;
you said it tasted cleaner, more refined.
And all those years I'd trimmed and grilled pork chops,

and roasted leg-of-pork, with apple sauce.
Pig's trotters you'd enjoy in restaurants.
Lucky you never craved a sucking pig.

On airlines too you'd go for Kosher meals:
put up your hand to signal from your seat
you'd asked for one. The old man next to you,

his *kippa* on his head, chatted away
in Yiddish, you in schoolboy German, till
puzzled, slightly hurt, he went back to his book.

A DREAM OF RICE

You brought home
four pounds of rice
in a large brown-paper bag.

I scooped up
a handful of round pearly grains
that fell through my fingers
and settled back with a gentle plink.

Down the side
you'd tucked a nest of tagliatelle –
paglia e fieno – specially for me,
which looked strangely misplaced.

I complained four pounds was too much,
one pound was all I normally bought;

and I forgot to thank you.

COURTING AT PATHSIDE

A stretch of river ran
through your small holding:
a tributary of the Hunyani.
You fired bricks from its red clay
and built yourself a house.

No swimming was allowed
even on the hottest day
for fear of crocodiles or worse:
the flatworm parasite, bilharzia.

So we picked our way
through scrubland to the house
and had parties there instead.
You greeted guests with 'Tally-Ho!',
Fed them your homemade *baklaïf*.

But your mother sickened,
developed tick-fever, took
to her bed and stayed there.
I felt I shouldn't be around,
shouldn't take her place.

I tried hard to keep away.

HOUSES

Our first, 'La Capannella', was a tumbledown house
with dynasties of spiders living in the cracks;
two thatched rondavels squatted in the garden,
and an imported peach tree shaded the front door.
You'd built a concrete table, welded wrought-iron gates.
At the back were mango and banana trees.

Our Mayfair flat in London had no trees.
You couldn't wait to get into a house
and redesign some new appropriate gates;
it would be smoothly plastered with no cracks.
You'd say: 'I want my very own front door,
a plot of land to work into a garden.'

In Penshurst ('Latymers') we shared a garden;
there was a lawn and mostly unfamiliar trees.
We had the pleasure of a private door.
But sadly we began to house
rancours that crawled like insects in the cracks.
From 'Penshurst Place' we'd hear the shutting of the Gates.

In Hampstead, on the Mount, there were no gates
and the Heath became our sit-in picnic garden;
though here the rifts had opened into serious cracks
and showed. Still, there were stately trees,
a top-floor flat more roomy than a house
with views right over London from our high-up door.

The men set down my piano at the door
and could have quite unhinged the spindly gates.
This was our first small terraced house
with fenced-in pocket-handkerchief of garden...
why did a branch stick out like gallows in the trees?
There was much pain in patching up the cracks.

The work of years has now repaired the cracks.
There's space for each of us behind this door.
You planted laurel hedges, aspen trees;
never got round to welding any gates.
When sickness struck, you'd look down and garden
in your mind, planning where to put a new greenhouse.

The garden's overgrown; no need of gates.
Your trees, like lifted arms, shelter my door.
In the soundless house, a voice inside me cracks.

CHAMPAGNE

Out of champagne cases (*Veuve Clicquot*)
we'd ordered for our wedding feast
you made a laundry box that's outlived you;
yellow then, now it's painted white.

I use it still despite its empty look
without your shirts and vests and woollen socks.
For the bedside lamp, we kept a mighty
jeroboam in sparkling green and gold.

Now all that fizz is but a memory
and the bubbles burst, I see a widow's
face trapped behind thick glass, fists
hammering, hammering to get out.

VILLANELLE

'To speak of woe that is in mariage'
Chaucer, *The Wife of Bath*

We always argued over trivial things:
Where to sit in restaurants, what to wear.
Regret and bitter taste is all that brings.

You'd reprimand me for my previous flings;
I'd criticise you for your vacant stare.
Why did we argue over trivial things?

You raged and sulked about my lost earrings
On honeymoon in Constitution Square.
Regret and bitter taste is all that brings.

Can couples guess it when they exchange rings
That rifts will come and widen, year on year?
How bagatelles can turn to serious things?

We stopped sharing our dreams, imaginings…
You knelt at Mass, while I stood up for prayer.
Regret and bitter taste is all that brings.

With age came love that softened many stings
(I see your bony face, your wispy hair).
Pity we quarrelled over trivial things.
Regret and bitter taste is all that brings.

THE LETTER

*'When one we love dies, there's no reason
to stop writing them letters.'*
Colette

It really is time to come back now,
a year-and-a-half's too long, much longer
than either of us intended; though I know
we both enjoyed your trips abroad, you,
your visits to other countries – one hundred
and three already notched up – and I,
not having to empty ashtrays, grill bacon,
iron shirts – some time to do nothing…
but now you can come back, I've had my rest,
and I promise to let you unwind
when you come in the door, not pounce on you
to mend the kettle or mow the lawn
or phone the man about the leaking roof:
and I promise to let you take your medicines
in any order you like and go to the doctor
with you, only if you want me to; and I won't
talk about poetry or show you my latest…
so you can safely come home and slip into bed;
I shan't say your breath smells of tobacco
or that your feet are unnaturally cold.

TOBACCO

It was the high-pitched chanting
of the auctioneer on the radio
(I could see him perched
over the neatly-packed bales)
that brought you back to me last night.

You had that song on tape:
'36..36..36½..37 IMPERIAL
37½..37½..38..38½.. B.A.T.
Watchoo gimme, watchoo gimme, 39?
39..39½..40 GALLAHER.' And
sometimes you mimicked it for me –
until your breath became too short.

Tobacco plants are a deep green,
they open like flower-petals,
their leaves delicately veined – you
drew them often for your magazine.

I'll put a *Nicotiana* on your grave
tonight, so you can smell
the sweet fragrance of the flowers.

ECCENTRIC

It could be a page
from any of your magazines,
rectangular, with its tilted globe logo

and carefully selected script
giving precise details of place of birth,
death, and dates; and underneath

something to identify the person:
'Traveller in body and mind.'
'Lover of language and languages.'

And we hung a string of figs
(which we thought the birds would enjoy)
across one side of it – this headstone,

much like a menhir really,
five-foot high, of Cumbrian riven slate,
more grey than blue-black in good light –

grey, a colour you liked and wore
and which suited you well –
remember your fur hat?

ABOUT SILENCE

Ce que l'on conçoit bien, s'énonce clairement.

Boileau (1636–1711)

DIPTYCH

About Silence

This morning I woke
to a new kind of silence –

not the silence
out of which music is made,

nor yet the silence
that precedes language,

or is like the chasm
between waves of the sea –

but an absolute silence
that engenders only itself,

as it might envelop
the windless moon

or deepen
the blackness of space...

a silence
of which I was born

and to which I shall add
my own silent note.

About Stillness

This morning I woke
to a new kind of stillness –

not the stillness that surrounds me
on a country walk,

nor the stillness of the house
just before dawn,

nor the stillness of the air
before a storm –

but the stillness of the self
that's now at ease

for having done with craving
things and place and praise

and (like the still motion
of dancers in a frieze

or of marble men and maidens
on an Attic urn)

is ready to join the still dance
when it will be my turn.

THE LAKE OF MY CHILDHOOD

is deep and green and still.
Three white clouds play
follow-my-leader in the sky.

On the water, three small boats go by;
there's a man, a woman and a child in each.
The man is the biggest. He rows.

In the first they wear no clothes,
in the second they're all dressed;
they've put on masks in the third.

Trees on the island (soft-focus, blurred)
are straight and silent. I'd given them names;
their trunks were for hiding behind.

Perhaps there's nothing more to find…
now all the boats have passed by,
I see only water, trees and sky.

CONVERSATION WITH AN ANGEL

On my way to Sainsbury's
I met an angel. He stood
relaxed, one foot and one wing
off the pavement, waiting
for me to pass. I stopped
to see if he needed anything; had he
lost his way? Could I help perhaps?
No, he lacked nothing, simply wanted
some contact with the world again;
he'd been human once and he craved
the bitter-sweet flavour...
Some angels were born – he explained –
others translated. Could I
become an angel? Was there a waiting list?
Not a chance for you, he laughed,
no one who has seen
an angel can ever become one.

LOOKING, STILL

Where shall I find you? Among stones?
On the red, red earth?
Beneath clumps of grasses?

Shall I took for you
under the green palms of oases?
At the well where women wash and gossip?

Or shall I seek you indoors
sitting cross-legged on the blue mosaics,
your drinking-bowl and sandals beside you?

And where shall I hear your voice?
In the memory? Among sounds not yet heard?
Or as a thunderous call above the crowd?

And your eyes, your almond eyes,
where shall I see them?
Only in the flat profile of processions?

What town or village will you inhabit?
Will you be walking in the heat of the sun,
or in the crystal light of the moon?

Will you know which doorway is for you?
And who in the deep indoors will be waiting for you?
That it could be me, with my stubborn longing?

COAT HANGER

After a drawing by Jasper Johns

1

It's wire, the colour of wire
and hangs on a knob.
It's got sloping shoulders
and a twisted neck. No,
the hook does not resemble a question.
Nobody's coat is on it; it's empty…
no, it's unoccupied.

2

This one's been covered with pink satin
and plumped out; there's a small bow
where the neck meets the shoulders.
A girl's first ballgown – red roses on a cream base –
hangs there, waiting … looped round the neck
a velvet sash and the cloth handles
of a puffy evening bag with its crest of pearls.

3

Every night
the black dress
on the wire hanger.

4

He sleeps but does not dream…
always he will see the coat hanger
behind the closed door.

5

In the morning
a question-mark
above a triangle.

999

I fell in love
and dialled 999
but no one came.

Then I fell out of love
and dialled 999
and still no one came.

Now, I'm neither in nor out of love
and helpers keep coming…
only, I'm not *there* to be rescued.

DUSTBIN

I look
for the wasted years,
those fat lean ones
I threw out
knowing full well
they were irreplaceable.

ORANGES

'Pack three oranges,' he'd say,
knowing the stretch of grass, waist-tall and prickly dry,
rising to a bore-hole, a windmill and a farm
would drain him and irritate his itchy nose.

Halfway up we'd find our flattish rocks
and rest there to get his breath.
He'd tie his white kerchief, pirate-like
round his head under his Panama, then peel
and break and hold out the segments on his palm.
The low buzz of insects deepened the silence.

Noon heat hurried us toward
the copse of swaying eucalyptus trees.
From that oasis we could see the road, the houses,
'Look,' he'd say, 'there's our garden; your bike.
You see things so much better from a distance.'

STARTING AGAIN

Snapshot, Bordighera 1949

And so we came back
to find Europe old and worn.
Our dead ones were not there to greet us.

Father, still young and eager to start again,
had plans for the future, but mother
would go no further into Italy,
only as far as this, a dozen fields
from the French border.

No she wouldn't go to Milan;
no, there was nothing there to salvage;
no, she didn't want to see the flat again –
how could she stare at what was no longer there.
She'd cursed it all so often and Mussolini with it.

She sat herself down
to look at the sea –
the sea might remember
and bring her a smell,
a sound, the feel of all those things
she'd hardly dared miss over there
in the dark/sunny country... and now,
maybe she'd find them again, here in Bordighera,
a dozen fields inside Italy,
in a small seaside town
of no great importance.

PRAYER FOR MY GRANDCHILD

Winter trees
naked
against the orange sunset;
across the park
the white, white moon
stuns the eyes
with brilliance.

One star
follows us –
me and this defenceless babe
under her crocheted shawl;
we meet from opposite ends
of our lives
and smile.

O Powers
protect her
from Princes that disturb
her sleep; from those others
who revert to frogs
and from juicy apples
proffered by witches.

Guide her
every step
through the Riding Hood forests,
for the sake of the smile
lifted to me here
in this lighted sunset
and those blue unclouded eyes.

A RENTED ROOM

This room, I see, does get the morning sun;
I like it well, especially the bay –
how the window overhangs the street.
And could I have a table here, to work?
I so love watching people passing by,
and horses' hoofs – their beat – it pleases me.
My piano could go there against the wall.
You don't mind music in the day, do you?
At night? I'll make no sound, I'm always out.
For I love company and coffee – strong.
I do have many friends; how kind of you
to let us have your salle for chamber works.
We meet and have a drink, then scrape away.
Of course, do come and listen if you wish.
But – please – no views; the critics can hold those.

What's that imposing inn across the street?
The sign looks blurred, I cannot read the name…
it is the *Schwarzer Adler*, you tell me;
and you the *Goldener Adler* – ah, that's good…
I see an eagle soaring near the sun,
becoming purest gold … speaking of which,
please take a month's rent, paid in advance.
I do not carry calling cards with me –
I'll write you down my name, my job, the date:
Franz Peter Schubert, song-writer, March 1821.

WHY CAN'T POETS HAVE SITTERS?

How simple it would be to *draw* your face –
The line that links your brow, your nose, your chin,
The honey-walnut colour of your skin –
If you were sitting here to speed my pace,
So that your *hereness* hardly left a trace
Of the other you I'm forced to hold within;
I'd see you a Picasso harlequin…
Or dress you up in purest silk and lace.

And other times I'd have you stay quite still,
A faraway expression in your eyes…
Pretend I'm recollecting in tranquil-
lity, but have you there to energise
My words and make them real, substantial,
Not mere abstractions, almost (say it!) lies.

A TIME TO GET UP AND GO

After Stevie Smith

Ariadne, Ariadne,
How much you grieve
Wrapped in your cloak of loose-weave
On that stone in Naxos.

Let him go, let him go,
Your golden hero;
He isn't worth it, and
Somewhere inside you, you know it.

You were cleverer always
(For who thought of the string?)
So do cease,
O cease your weeping.

Ingeniously you're using it now
To hang out your hankies each day,
Rinsed of the tears and the pain,
Again and again and again.

Now dye them bright colours, Ariadne,
Hoist them to the mast,
Wave Theseus away in the past,
And *do* do it fast.

For women abandoned
With nothing much to do
Are not a pretty sight; and
Though Bacchus may turn up tonight

(And he's a jollier fellow)
Resolve upon your own thing;
Climb on that ship, Ariadne,
Sail off and sing, O sing!

VOID

This morning in the mirror I wasn't there –
I did see you behind me though, lying
on the bed breathing quietly, and the tallboy,
the two doors and the picture – but not me.

I thought: this emptiness will pass,
I'll try again later – catch myself
unawares, go past casually, sideways
maybe, and look swiftly, not stare.

But in the evening there was still no me.
As I searched the depths of the mirror
it began to liquefy, the silver hardness of it
melting to become a surging sea

where a vast whale gurgled and gasped for breath,
rasping through its blowhole. From the harpoon-
wound
the slimy blue-black blood trickled, slowly at first
then spreading to cover the whole mirror.

I could no longer see, but I heard a distant whine
(the frequency too high for ears at normal times)
but now a threnody, a dirge, a long lament...
and my own voice keening with the whale's.

DESERT LANDSCAPE WITH ONE FIGURE

The man walks bent forward,
straw hat tied under his chin;
threadbare jacket, crumpled trousers.
As he lifts each foot out of the sand
a well forms
which closes up again behind him,

He doesn't often scan the horizon
for other figures like himself:
he must preserve energy to keep moving,
to keep thinking, to concentrate his mind
on walking, on thinking.

In the day the sun
beats down on his back;
at night cold winds whistle
through his coat, his punctured vest.
He shivers and hugs himself.

He digs a trench with his hands
and sleeps in it pulling
the blanket of sand over his body.
He's snug there and forgets...

Sometimes the sky is friendly,
the stars are eyes that watch over him.
At daybreak there's colour in the sky,
it gives energy, hope; at sunset streaks of violet
are like drawings-in, like endings.

He walks on but stops now and then
to sift sand from palm to palm for a game.
He drinks water he carries with him; counts days,
counts dunes; turns away from the green
in the distance
for fear it may not really be there.

FJORDS

I dreamed of fjords
I saw from a slow ship,
with the long summer light on them,
their water deep and dark.

In the sheer cliff caverns
lived the northern gods
(whose unfamiliar names were told me
and I feared on waking I'd forget).

My companions dived off the deck,
swam boldly circling the ship
and waving to me called out:
'Jump in, don't be afraid, it's warm.'

I stayed on deck
gripping the railing;
I knew I couldn't swim
but I could look and listen.

Endlessly I hear them calling:
'Jump in, jump, it's warm.'

COMING HOME

'How goodly are thy tents, O Jacob'
    Numbers 24: 5

The tent of Jacob
opened up for me today –
though it was never shut,
its canvas flapping in the wind.

I bend very low
to step through the sandy entrance,
but once inside
I stretch to my full height.

I come back humbly,
tired out by the long journey,
the sojourn among strangers
in their kind of habitation.

I've learnt
of unfamiliar places,
of other ways of being,
of otherness…

Here in the tent
I'm not asked to explain;
the musty smell of the dock
is but a memory.

It's a jubilant setting free;
a coming out of Egypt once again.
And the sea is there to plunge into,
to wash me clean.

WINDWARD ISLANDS

No, not a banana comes to mind
but a wind that swells the sails
of a two-masted schooner;

that clears the skies of clouds,
of greynesses – even the silver-lined –
and makes openings, vistas, possibilities;

lets you see the tops of mountains,
sweeps away jetsam, lets flotsam go,
and gets to the core; reveals

the bare sand... and the ship sets off
on its final journey, dwarfed by the wind's might,
out, way out, until it drops from sight.

MISSING OUT THE *PAUL JONES*

I can see her now,
that girl out there on deck,
watching and awed under the stars,
on a black-and-silver night, as the ship
flees the ever-chasing moon
huge and low on the horizon.

Now she's seeking to arrange
the patterns on the spumy wake;
with the brine itching her nostrils
and tingling her soft neck,
as she bends her head backwards
to see the stars wink and beckon.

From the lounge, the sound of a dance band,
voices, excitement… someone shouts:
'Come inside, it's the *Paul Jones* next.'
But she's already spinning with the stars,
partner to the thrusting sea. So she says:
'I'll miss out the *Paul Jones* tonight.'

LEAVING

If you ask me to leave
I shall go quietly by the front door,
crossing the threshold on my own two feet.

And I shall go looking
for the long low pink house of my childhood,
by the river with many bends.

The river was in sunlight
when first I looked at it
through the paling of the bridge high up.

Later I saw a patch of deep shade under the willow,
and I shuddered for thinking
there I might drown myself.

Now again I've found the pink house
and I'm moving in.

The rooms are smaller,
uncluttered, silent.

If you knock at my door
I may not even hear you...

The river is just below my window.

TRIUMPHANT

Cross-legged, she sits on stacked pillows
enthroned on the high-bed of birth,
the baby in the crook of her leg.

She holds court exuberantly, telling
whoever passes by and will listen
of her five-hour joyful ordeal, still soaked

in the sour sweat of labour; her blood
deep-staining the sheets; the baby still warm
from the womb's warmth and the cord uncut.

Rising and falling her clean voice traces
the stages in the journey of separation
and enfolds the naked infant who sleeps on.

FOR HUGO

in memoriam Rabbi Hugo Gryn
died London, 18 August 1996

Why do I think of you as my own friend?
I met you only once but sensed the grace
And wholeness of a mind that could transcend
All bars of colour, background, creed and race.

You lit up, every week, that tortuous 'maze'
With parables and stories ages old
But shining new; and with a self-turned phrase
You gave us something good to keep and hold.

You saw your father die, your brother too,
And countless others. Yet you came out pure,
Determined it would not embitter you
But teach you, teach us all, how to endure.

May God *you* never left despite that hell
Receive you now, receive and guard you well.

CITY LIFE

Tracey's Ansafone

Sorry I can't come to the phone right now, I'm working.
If you'd just like to stare into my eyes, say ONE.
If you'd like to stare into my eyes and have a chat, say TWO.
If you'd like to have a chat and a sloppy kiss, say THREE.
If you'd like a sloppy kiss and a cuddle, say FOUR.
If you'd like kinky games, say FIVE.
If you'd like kinky games plus extras, say SIX.
If you're going all the way, say SEVEN.
If you're just playing the fool, say NOTHING
and bloody get off the line
so someone else can have a turn.

Coffee-Shop

They sit together.
He's on his mobile;
several times she looks at him
appealing…
He's on his mobile
laughing, gesticulating.
They get up to go;
with his free hand
(he's on his mobile)
he picks up a shopping-bag;
she picks up the rest.
He starts walking
'talk to you soon.'
She turns him
in the direction he should be going.

Sloane Street

CHANEL
COACH
LOUIS VUITTON
FERRAGAMO
BROWN'S
OILILY

and on the pavement
sitting on newspapers
middle-aged man
upturned cap
bottle at his feet.
Scribbled on cardboard:
'Homeless and hungry.'

BRUNO MAGLI
GIORGIO ARMANI
FERRE
NICOLE FARHI
YVES ST. LAURENT
PIED À TERRE

and on the pavement
sitting on newspapers
youngish woman
baby at the breast
plastic mug for *droppings*.

Scribbled on cardboard:
'My baby's sick.'

LATE SUMMER WALK

For Ted Burford

Your fingers in mine are skeins of silk;
your voice is quiet, as though,
already, it had drifted away.

Intermittent rays of sun
burn my neck; my hands tingle.
Our steps are slow,

intent on prolonging time
and fixing it on a tape
to be played again and again.

But now, still, silk threads
link and distance us
like the strings of summer kites.

Look, the leaves are turning yellow;
I move my head imperceptibly
in the direction of your going.

PASSING THROUGH

I've seen
the crystal rings of Saturn,
your face round as the moon,
poppies the colour of apricots.

I've heard
the roar of the sea,
Schubert's 'Great C major'
and a baby's first da-da.

I've smelt
fresh-ground coffee, new-washed clothes
and the well in the pillow
where your head rested.

I've tasted
peach syrup,
spinach in cheese pastry;
food fried golden on the bottom of pans.

I've touched
the silk of Kashmiri skin,
the warm ivory of piano keys;
polished stone, wood-bark.

And I've known
the mind soar,
the imagination take flight
and break the speed of light.

All this
passing through just once,
just once as me
and never again.

THOUGHTS ON EMPEROR HIROHITO'S FUNERAL

I have a friend
who's learning Japanese

I shan't be learning Japanese
though I like their ideograms

My father had a friend
who never came back from Burma

He'd learnt some Japanese –
words for hunger, thirst, bellyache

They nailed him to a door
and cut him into quarters

I can see that – man on door –
as an ideogram for torture.

BOSNIA JINGLE

I'm bombing
You're shooting
I'm sniping
You're looting

You're bombing
I'm firing
You're wounding
I'm crying

We're aiding
They're raiding
You're bleeding
I'm pleading

We're blasting
They're fasting
I'm limbless
He's headless

I'm shelling
You're yelling
NO – you're shelling
I'm yelling

They're strifing
He's knifing
We're laughing
WE'RE LAUGHING

You're signing
We're dining
They're tabling
I'm labelling

I'm praying
Who's listening
He's screaming
I'm beaming

They're digging
We're chanting
They're planting
I'm dying

'...and don't forget to water my tomatoes'

Now I've reached the age you were
when grandfather came back that morning
to say they wanted the women too,
and would you pack a small case
and he'd go to the *Cay Ancha* to call a coach.

He was sweating and trembling while he waited
for you to tell Petrizza, the Greek girl, to help herself
to food under the wire mesh in the larder,
put the white covers over the chairs,
and remember to water the tomatoes.

Now I've reached the age you were that July
when you arrived at the Air Force Headquarters,
dazed, hardly able to greet
the many you knew from the *Juderia*
who were equally baffled – what are we doing here?

That night you all slept together
on the floor – you'd slept on the floor
at your uncle's in Izmir, but that was wooden
and it had been fun – here it's marble
and other people's limbs are poking into you.

                    In your restless sleep
you hear the cannonade of 1912; the Italians
are ousting the Turks and taking the island.
But they're soon friendly – they set up a bandstand
in the middle of the *Mandraki*. Every Sunday

Cay Ancha – wide street, avenue
Juderia – Jewish quarter
Mandraki – promenade on the sea front

snippets of *Tosca*, *Rigoletto*, *Aïda* fill the air;
dancing-masters with half-size fiddles
teach the girls the newest steps.
And haven't they knighted your husband:
Cavaliere Ufficiale della Corona d'Italia?

They'd called Rhodes '*l'Isola delle Rose*'
(how beautiful as a rose it still is)
and for five hundred years you'd lived
in your model-Jerusalem – '*La pequeña Yerushalaïm*' –
protected by the Turks, unmolested by the Greeks,

tolerated by the Knights-Hospitallers, even,
whose huge cannon-balls
surrounding their fort by the harbour
I'd sit on as a child, wondering
with vague apprehension what they could be.

Next morning you see *l'Hermana Fasana* defecate
in a corner of the vast hall. Toothlessly old
and with her stick lost in the mêlée,
she couldn't make it
to the toilets on the third floor.

What you wouldn't give right now
for a nice cup of Turkish coffee
to dislodge the rusty rakes in your throat…
but comes a shout in the barking language
you don't understand, to stand up, get in line,

strip down to your knickers. The shame, oh the shame!
In front of all these people: men, children?
The butcher from down the road, the electrician
who came only yesterday to mend a fuse?
The posh ladies from the villas on the hillside?

Cavaliere Ufficiale della Corona d'Italia – Knight Officer of the Crown
of Italy
l'Hermana Fasana – Sister Fasana, term of endearment for old
women in the ghetto

When we went together to the Turkish Baths
I saw your well-formed body, baby-clean,
skin smooth and unblemished…yet at home
you'd make me stand in a corner
facing the wall, when you got undressed.

Then ordered to walk in single file and in silence
to the three petrol-tankers waiting
down in the harbour…how lovely
to breathe fresh air again though,
after the stinks and the sweats of the night.

You wonder how long
before you're back home; will Petrizza
manage to look after the house, will she
steal much?… But where are the others:
Tante Diamante, l'oncle Josef, Norma and the twins?

They must be in the second or the third tanker…
Luckily grandfather's here with his arm round you.
Together you stare at the receding quayside;
neither dares tell the other of the feeling
you'll never see your house or your island again.

I went to look for your house, Granny.
It's there, next door to the Keila de la Paz;
derelict, its imposing outside staircase crumbling.
The Greek woman who'd moved in forthwith, anxious
to assure me everything was hers: tables, divans, rugs…

You sail for ten choppy days,
picking up Jews from nearby islands:
relations from Kos. You notice the hem
of your black satin dress is badly torn
and your crocheted collar has yellowed.

Keila de la Paz – Temple of Peace

SS officers in Piraeus
flog grandfather with a horsewhip,
pull you by the hair and the young women
by their breasts. Beat the elderly
with their own sticks and throw them away.

Then to Athens station. You'd been told
the Parthenon is here – city of Socrates,
a great man who gave light to the world.
But the trains are dark, windowless, light
filtering in only through cracks.

Now my body aches with yours –
my lower back's locked, my ankles swollen;
an outsize hammer thumps at my temples.
The lining of my stomach presses on a cavity.
Weals in my throat stop me swallowing.

Fourteen days later you've arrived
at you don't know where;
and the sign over the gate tells you nothing.
You enter block twenty with other women
and collapse on a straw-mattressed bunk.

In the morning a barking SS woman
shaves your head; the long greyish-brown hair
you'd let me comb at night, falls on the cement.
She forbids you to pick up a piece
and holds a mirror to your face, laughing.

News item: the storehouse
near Auschwitz where hair was piled
before sending it off to stuff
mattresses, pillows and cushions,
is to be turned into a disco.

The days and nights blur into each other.
There's a call for time to go to the shower unit.
You're given a bar of soap and a towel
and told to leave your clothes outside;
many, many others go – with you.

Inside there's a smell like when Petrizza
used to change the gas cylinders. This is no *hammam*!
People are stampeding towards the doors,
lifting little children up away from the gas jets.
You sing a loud *'el Dio es Grande'* and fall, still singing.

hammam – Turkish bath
el Dio es Grande – God is Great

BLACK THOMAS

After a visit to the Imperial War Museum's
Holocaust Exhibition

Thomas the tank engine's face is black.
He's been to hell, to hell and back,
swerving and swaying on a thin narrow track.

His eyes are flames and his mouth is red.
In the wagon there's straw, wet straw for a bed;
but no cattle or sheep, just people instead.

As he reaches the gate there's a distant bell,
but no sound is heard, not a shout or a yell.
They've all gone quiet with the silence of hell.

And he puffs with a smoke that's yellowy black
to match that column up there at the back
that's rising and rising from a chimney-stack.

And when he's delivered these women and men
he goes back for more, again and again,
again and again, and again and again.

MY SKULL IS TURNED UP ON A DIG

'Here we have the skull
of a woman who lived
circa one thousand nine hundred and eighty AD.
We can tell the sex
by the small size of the cranium.
As you know, female skull dimensions
have increased considerably
over the past two thousand years.
We can deduce she was of medium build
and of Mediterranean origin.
These widely spaced sockets could indicate
large eyes and a roundish nose.
We see a tall brow with sunken temples.

Look, here, where my pencil points –
it's as if the parietal bones
never quite knit together,
prolonging the fontanelle effect.
It is said (though this is strictly
unscientific) that such people
tend to be overly attached
to their childhood, their mother.
Now you examine it
and write up your notes.
Give it back when you've finished.
I'd like to put it on my desk
as a *memento mori*.'

FROM CHILDHOOD
TONGUES

ABOUT TRANSLATION

A language is more than just an agglomeration of words, a rulebook of grammar: it's a way of living, of responding to the world around one, of eating, of sleeping, of making love, of bringing up children, of relating to others. It's also the sound the words make when spoken; it's the connotations and the echoes those words set up, the pictures they create in the mind.

I translate for the sheer joy of it. No doubt because the 'way of being' of each of the three other European languages I speak, takes me back through a tunnel of years to Italy where I was born, to France where I first knew the pleasure of serious learning at the Lycée Molière, and to the family circle where uncles and aunts and friends spoke that fifteenth-century Spanish – the language of Lope de Vega – which Jews expelled from the Iberian peninsula during the Inquisition, preserved to this day as *Ladino*.

I love the elegance and intellectual rigour of French; the passion and intensity of Spanish; the bell-like clarity and graceful emotion of Italian. If I want to change my mood I switch to another language, *'et ça y est'*.

And what of English, the language I'm translating into? That's the one I must know best. It's a language of endless subtlety, infinite possibilities; flexible, open-ended, and imbued with humour. It has been enriched all through its history by invaders and settlers; by the galleons carrying cargoes of words from the far-flung Empire, as now, with the speed of flight, from the United States and from every other place on the planet.

I never understood why it is written that God cursed men with a plurality of tongues. Rather, it's a blessing. Long live Babel, I say, and get to work on a translation.

THE MEMORY OF YOU

I sense your memory detaching itself
from my mind like an old print;
your outline
already has no head
and an arm has dissolved, like in those
melancholy transfers
children at school place on a page,
and which afterwards are found as a smudgy stain
in a forgotten book.

When I squeeze your body
I get the feeling it's made of rag.
You talk to me and your voice
sounds so distant
I can only just hear you. Besides
I no longer believe you.
As for me, I have recovered
from my old passion:
how, I ask myself, could I have loved you –
so useless, so vain,
so insubstantial that in under a year
of holding you in my arms
you're dissolving like a swirl of smoke;
and you're already fading like an ancient drawing –
your memory detaching itself from my mind
like an old print.

NICOLÁS GUILLÉN (1902–1989), Cuba

FIRING SQUAD

They're going to shoot
a man whose arms are tied.
Four soldiers
are ready to fire.
They're four sullen
soldiers
who are also bound
like the trussed man
they'll fell to the ground

'Can you get away?'
'I can't run.'
'They're going to fire.'
'I'm undone.'
'Maybe the rifles aren't loaded...'
'They've six bullets of fierce lead.'
'Maybe they'll turn round instead.'
'You're a fool with wool in your head.'

They've fired.
(How was it they could fire?)
They've killed.
(How was it they could kill?)
They were four sullen soldiers
standing on a line
and a gentleman officer gave them a sign,
lowering his sword:
they were four soldiers
bound
like the trussed man
the four of them felled to the ground.

NICOLÁS GUILLÉN

SONG

There's more wisdom in your belly
than in your head –
in your muscles too.

Such is
the strong black grace
of your naked body.

Yours is the sign of the wild,
with your crimson chains,
your bangles of beaten-gold,
and that slithery crocodile
swimming in the Zambesi of your eyes.

NICOLÁS GUILLÉN

WRITTEN IN GREEN INK

Green ink makes gardens, meadows, forests,
foliage out of which letters sing,
words that are trees,
sentences that are green constellations.

Let my words, O white one, fall and cover you
like a shower of leaves on a field of snow,
like ivy around a statue,
like the ink on this page.

Arms, waist, neck, breasts,
forehead clear as the sea,
the nape cool as a wood in autumn,
teeth that bite on a blade of grass.

Your body is studded with green emblems
like the body of a tree coming into leaf.
Don't worry about so many bright scars;
look at the sky with its green tattoo of stars.

OCTAVIO PAZ (1914–1998), Mexico

FAREWELL

1

From deep down inside you, and all curled up,
a child, as sad as I am, is looking at us.

For the life that will burn in his veins
our lives will have to be embittered.

For those hands, sprung from your hands,
my hands will have to commit murder.

For his eyes open on to the earth
I shall see tears in yours one day.

2

I do not want him, my love.

So that nothing should embitter us,
that nothing should bind us.

Neither the word your mouth sweetened,
nor what words did not say.

Neither the banquet of love we never had,
nor your sobs by the window.

3

(I love the love of sailors
that kiss and are gone.

They leave giving a promise.
They don't ever return.

In every port a woman's hoping,
the sailors kiss and are gone.

One night they lie down with death
on the bed of the sea.)

4

I love the love that shares out
its kisses, its bed, its bread.

Love that can be eternal
or can be fleeting.

Love that wants to free itself
in order to love again.

An exquisite love that draws near.
An exquisite love tnat draws away.

5

No longer will my eyes find enchantment in yours,
no longer will my pain find solace near you.

But wherever I go I shall see your look
and wherever you walk you'll carry my sorrow.

I was yours, you were mine. What else? Together we made
a bend in the road where love passed.

I was yours, you were mine. You'll be your loved one's
who will reap what I've sown in your garden.

I'm leaving. I'm sad, but I'm always sad.
I've just come from your embrace. I don't know where I'm going.

From your heart a child says farewell.
And I say to him *fare well.*

PABLO NERUDA (1904–1973), Chile

INWARDNESS

Be good, O my sorrow, and keep yourself calm.
You clamoured for the evening; here it is; it falls:
A blanket of darkness envelops the town,
To some it brings worry, to others balm.

Now the vile human crowd joins the fray
Whipped on by Pleasure, that pitiless brute,
And goes gathering guilt at the flattering feast,
My sorrow, give me your hand; come this way,

Far from them, see the dead years in faded gown,
Over the balconies in the sky, lean down,
Regret surface smiling from the deep;

See, under an arch, the dying sun asleep,
And, like a long shroud dragging from the East,
Listen, my dear, hear the gentle night creep.

CHARLES BAUDELAIRE (1821–1867), France:
'Recueillement'

STAYING IN

Let's stay at home tonight,
Just the two of us, intimately;
You've so often longed for the half-light
Of evening: here it is, it falls soundlessly.

While the riff-raff go pleasure-seeking
Down in Soho and Leicester Square
In pubs, clip joints, arcades reeking
Of sweat, pee and puke, come over here

Away from all that; give me your hand,
Stand at the window, see the dead years
How droll they look in their faded gowns
And all our might-have-beens dressed as clowns.

We'll enjoy the night itself and the sky,
You my sorrow, and I.

CHARLES BAUDELAIRE:
'Recueillement' (modern-dress version)

LOVERS TALKING

In the old park, deserted and stiff with snow,
Two shapes went by a little while ago.

Their lips are limp and their eyes are dead,
And you can scarcely hear what they said.

In the old park, deserted and stiff with snow,
Two shades spoke of long ago.

'D'you remember how love held us in thrall?'
'Would you really expect me to recall?'

'Does the mere mention of my name set you a-glow?
Do you still see my soul in dreams?' 'No.'

'Ah! Those bright days of love inexpressible
When our mouths would touch!' 'It's possible.'

'How huge hope was, how blue the sky!'
'Hope's vanquished, fled to where illusions lie.'

So through the crazed oats they walked,
And the night alone heard them as they talked.

PAUL VERLAINE (1844–1896), France

UNTITLED

In the hourless forest
They're felling a great tree.
A vertical, bole-shaped
Emptiness shivers
Near the laid-out trunk.

Seek out, birds, seek out
The spot where your nests were
In that high reach memory
While the whispering lasts.

JULES SUPERVIELLE (1884–1960), France

OBSESSED WITH SOLITUDE

I eat a little supper by the lighted window.
In the room it's already dark and you can see in the sky.
Outside the quiet streets lead
after a while to open country.
I eat and look into the sky – who knows how many women
are eating at this hour – my body's quiet;
work dulls my body and every woman.

Out there, after supper, the stars will come out
and touch the earth on the wide plain. The stars are alive,
but not worth these cherries I eat alone.
I see the sky, but I know that among the rusty roofs
some lamp is lit already, and there are noises coming from below.
A great gulp and my body relishes the life
of plants and rivers, and feels remote from everything.
You need only a little silence for each thing to be set
in its true place, like this, like my own body.

Each thing stands out before my senses
which accept it without fuss: a hum of silence.
In the darkness I can know each thing
as I know that my blood courses through my veins.
The plain is a great rush of water through the grasses,
a supper of all things. Each plant and each stone
lives in stillness. I listen to my food nourish the veins
of each thing that lives on this plain.

Night does not matter. That square of sky
murmurs me away from all noises, and a thin star
struggles in the void, far from the food,
from the houses, other. But it's not self-sufficient
and needs too many companions. Here in the dark, alone,
my body's quiet and feels master of itself.

CESARE PAVESE (1908–1950), Italy

FROM 'XENIA'

Dear little insect
nicknamed 'fly', for some reason,
this evening when it was almost dark
and I was reading Deutero-Isaiah
you reappeared beside me,
but you hadn't your glasses on,
so you couldn't see me
and nor could I without that gleam
recognise you in the gloom.

For the hereafter, we'd been practising
a whistle, some sign of recognition.
I'm trying out variations on it, hoping
we're all dead already without knowing it.

Listening was your only way of seeing.
The telephone bill is much reduced.

Your brother died young; you were
the tousled girl who looks at me
posing out of an oval portrait.
He wrote unpublished, unheard music,
now buried in a trunk or sent off
to be pulped. Maybe someone's reinventing it
unwittingly, if what's written is written.
I loved him without ever knowing him.
No one remembered him apart from you.
I made no enquiries: now it's pointless.
Other than you, I'm the only one for whom
he existed. But it's possible, you know,
to love a shadow, shadows ourselves.

EUGENIO MONTALE (1896–1981), Italy

FROM 'SATURA'

Rhymes are more tiresome than
the Sisters of Charity: they knock on the door
and insist. It's impossible to push them away
but provided they stay outside, they're tolerable.
Any decent poet holds them at arm's length
(rhymes, that is), he hides them, cheats, tries
smuggling. But those zealots burn
with passion and sooner or later (rhymes and old nags)
will go on knocking and they never let up.

EUGENIO MONTALE

YOU CAN STILL HEAR THE SEA

It's many nights now I can still hear the sea,
swaying gently, back and forth, over the smooth sands.
The echo of a voice shut away in the mind,
rising out of the past; and so too
this constant crying of gulls: perhaps
of birds from the towers that April
drives towards the plains. Already
you were near me with that voice;
and I wish that now the echo of a memory of me
would come to you as well,
like that dark murmur of the sea.

SALVATORE QUASIMODO (1901–1968), Italy

NOW THAT DAY IS BREAKING

The night is ended and the moon
dissolves slowly into the clear sky,
sets in the canals.

In this flat land September
is so lively, the fields are as green
as our southern valleys in spring.

I've left my friends,
I've hidden my heart inside the ancient walls,
to be alone and think of you.

How much further than the moon
you seem, now that day is breaking
and horses' hooves beat on the flagstones.

SALVATORE QUASIMODO

ACKNOWLEDGEMENTS

Some of these poems have previously appeared in the following publications: *Acumen, Daily Express, European Judaism, The Jewish Quarterly, The Observer, Other Poetry, Outposts* and *Resurgence*; and in four anthologies: *Messages*, compiled by Naomi Lewis (Faber & Faber, 1985); *Poetry Street 1*, compiled by David Orme and James Sale (Longman, 1991); *Home*, edited by Kathleen McPhilemy (Katabasis, 2000); and *Dark as a Midnight Dream*, compiled by Fiona Waters (Evans Bros, 2000). 'Conversation with an Angel' was broadcast on the BBC TV children's programme *Jackanory*.

Every effort has been made to contact the copyright holders of the poems translated by Wanda Barford in 'From Childhood Tongues'. Two of the three poems by Nicolás Guillén, 'Tu Recuerdo' and 'Madrigal', are from *Poesías de Amor Hispanoamericanas*, edited by Mario Benedetti (Instituto del Libro, La Habana, Cuba, 1969); the third, 'Fusilamiento', is from *El Son Entero* (Editorial Losada S.A., Buenos Aires, 1952). The poem by Pablo Neruda, 'Farewell', is from *Crepusculario* (© Pablo Neruda, 1923, and Fundación Pablo Neruda). The poem by Cesare Pavese, 'Mania di solitudine', is from *Lavorare stanca* (Le poesie di Cesare Pavese © Giulio Einaudi editore). The poem by Octavio Paz, 'Eserito con tinta verde', is from *The Collected Poems 1957–1987*, edited by Eliot Weinberger (Carcanet Press, 2001). The poems by Salvatore Quasimodo, 'Ora che sale il giorno' and 'S'ode ancora il mare', are from *Tutte Le Poesie* (© Arnoldo Mondadori Editore SpA, Milano, 1979). The poems by Eugenio Montale, untitled ones from 'Xenia', and 'Le Rime' from 'Satura', are from *Lo Specchio* (© Arnoldo Mondadori Editore SpA, Milano, 1971). The untitled poem by Jules Supervielle, 'Dans la forêt sans heures...', is from *Forçat innocent* (© Éditions Gallimard, 1930 and 1969).